# American Nobility: The Threston Family
# by Roger McHugh

Historic Genealogy Books Inc
New York, NY

ISBN-13: 978-0692422557
ISBN-10: 0692422552

# Forward

As a professional genealogist most projects come and go, and, while every family has their own unique story; very few stick with you and, compel you continue to research long after the paid assignment ends; and, this was my case with the Threston family. This is truly one of the only families that has compelled me on to further research on my own. Not only is the surname very rare and ancient as mentioned and, documented in my first book on the family with Dr. Amy Lynn; but, this is the only family I've encountered that had extremely old (traceable) documentation going back almost 1,000 years who ranged from Knights Templars and nobility to Irish land gentry to teachers and politicians and modern day engineers, lawyers, writers, publishers, teachers, health professionals and even fashion models. And, it goes to prove how poorly history was documented and how slanted it was written for the ages with those in power controlling who and what became what we (until now) have accepted as the only "correct" history.

The fact remains, I am convinced this is not the only family that has been overlooked by history, but, I was driven to bring the Threston family to light by the written word for future reference and generations to come based on the points I mentioned in the above paragraph. In particular, the Threstons of Plymouth, Pennsylvania. I find it utterly fascinating that such a prominent family of this small town was almost forgotten, and, while this may prove to be of no interest to anyone outside of myself or the Threston family, I did in fact want to make sure that somehow, some way I did my part to bring this part of the family into light for the rest of the world to see.

I have documented all information to eliminate all arguments about speculation, hearsay and being accused of making things up as was accused by some in the genealogy field. It is unfortunate that professional jealousy or other types of jealousy prevail, however, since each of evidence is now properly documented it will be hard for genealogists and the rest of the world to dispute my findings.

And while I stated this on my website, I want to reiterate my experience with Wikipedia. It should be noted and included that when John J. Threston was presented to Wikipedia for inclusion, the original inclusion was revoked (and John J. Threston deleted) due to the argument that this case did not exist and/or the importance of the case. It is stated for the record that the McLean vs Bowman case was indeed real and can be found in newspapers such as The Wilkes Barre Record and, books as well as government records, specifically Records of the U.S. House of Representatives RG.233.62.House 62nd Congress Finding aid prepared by Office of Art and Archives, Office of the Clerk, U.S. House of Representatives. Once again showing that Wikipedia is not always accurate or correct even though often cited. It is a shame that Wikipedia is operated by non-historians and others without knowledge and allowed to govern what is included.

This decision also effected other inclusions that also have historical significance such as Sir Edward Threston who is a documented Knights Templar. Additionally it should be noted for the record that this is not "sour grapes" on part of the researchers or the Threston family. Other far more high profile individuals such as professional golfer Fuzzy Zoeller had defamatory remarks made about him in Wikipedia, and, John Seigenthaler suffered character assassination on Wikipedia thus proving the point Wikipedia is hardly a true source of honest, correct and real information.

The information provided has been researched and documented in a way that all sources are made publicly available with the hope that one day the Threston family will take their rightful place in true historical records and accounting that are fact based. In the meantime the good people of the Plymouth (Pennsylvania) Historical Society have graciously accepted the information provided on this website and have expressed their appreciation of the information and documentations found here. They will add the information to their records and database in due time.

Finally, I must give both credit and thanks to Tina Rinaldi, great granddaughter of John J. Threston, granddaughter of Evelyn Threston Zoransky, and, daughter of Anne Marie Zoransky Rinaldi, who aided in my research and writing of this book. Tina is more widely known by her pen name T.R. Threston, and, she is a highly accomplished travel writer and publisher, and, is currently working on a historical fiction novel "Tharston Manor" for which I was originally hired to research the Threston family in the 1550s. It has been an honor to work with someone of her caliber and she made the experience enjoyable and gave invaluable personal insight to her family.

- Roger McHugh

# Family Trees

I am only listing (known) family members until the grandchildren of John J. Threston of Plymouth, Pennsylvania and Peter Threston of Plymouth, Pennsylvania. This is out of the respect for privacy of current living members of the family, however, a simple Internet search will certainly bring current members of this family (who are very impressive in their own right) to the curious reader or researcher.

It needs to be said that like nearly every family tree there are gaps and missing information and, with the exception of kings and queens and their immediate families this holds true to most family genealogy at this time. With more and more people turning to DNA we can hope to close this gap, but, for now we must rely on written documentation, and, that is why there will be great gaps in this family tree.

# John J. Threston Family

## Gentleman John Threston

### Birth 13 Nov 1872 in Plymouth, Luzerne, Pennsylvania, USA

### Death 24 Sep 1939 in Wilkes-Barre, Luzerne, Pennsylvania, USA

John J. Threston was born on November 13, 1872, he was the son of Richard Threston, who was from County Mayo, Ireland. It needs to be noted as it was in my first book with Dr. Amy Lynn that the Threston name has varied over the centuries and by country. In Ireland, the "h" was dropped and the family became Treston. This is due to the Irish/Gaelic pronunciation of the English language that the letter "H" often disappears. The Irish speak in a way that is quite heavy on the R's and passive on soft T's, and, the H becomes silent, for example: Three becomes Tree, and, Threston becomes Treston.

Richard Threston was Richard Treston in Ireland, and, he was part of the Treston gentry that owned thousands of acres of land in counties Sligo and Mayo. (Further information can be obtained by exploring Griffiths Valuation of Ireland.)

It also needs to be further stated that Richard Threston, father of John J. Threston left Ireland to return to England where all the children, expect for John J. Threston were born. John J. Threston was the first American born member of the Threston clan (at least on this part of the branch of the family tree.) There is hard evidence that other Threston family members were in the Americas and were part of the American revolution as documentation will show later in this book.

RICHARD THRESTON (FATHER)
JOHN J. THRESTON --I
VERONICA BURKE THRESTON (MOTHER)

John J. Threston married Mary Margaret McLaughlin Smith. She was known as Margaret. They married in Plymouth, Pennsylvania on Christmas day in 1895. The news clipping (page) and reference source show the registration for a marriage license.

at the Bloomingdale M. E. church. Interment in Bloomingdale cemetery.

The following marriage licenses were granted yesterday: William J. Lewis and Marie Phillips, of Wilkes-Barre; A. P. Harrison and Maggie E. Pritchard, of Plymouth; Conrad Seiple, of Brown's Corners, Pa., and Stella Pringle, of Plymouth township; John Threston, of Plymouth, and Margaret Smith, of Edwardsville; William H. Miller and Lena M. King, of Pittston; John J. Griffin and Gretta Jones, of Alden; George Maher and Augusta Chamberlin, of Nanticoke; S. V. McCracken and Sarah Wheeler, of Wilkes-Barre; William H. Knittle and Laura Smith, of Wilkes-Barre.

News clipping source:   The Scranton Republican (Scranton, Pennsylvania) 25 December 1895 Page 8

John J. Threston held many political positions within the town of Plymouth, Pennsylvania. It should be noted that many of the positions do not have the same esteem in today's world as they did in the late 1800s and early 1900s. However, in that time period, these positions were highly regarded and important, and, the fact that John J. Threston held his first elected position at age 30 was an achievement all in itself. It also tells about the upstanding background and reputation of the entire Threston family.

In 1902 (at age 30) John J. Threston was elected both as Town Auditor and as Justice of the Peace. The news clippings (pages ) give solid evidence of these facts, and, in the case of Justice of the Peace, the clipping shows a list of the other applications for the job who were who were Michael Mooney, Bernard Williams, William Kulp, W.T. Sutliffe and Daniel Driscoll.

In 1911, Threston added Truancy Officer to his list of political careers, and, in 1917, he was enlisted to enroll young men in the military for World War I, which included members of his own family, nephews, Richard George Threston, Terrance Threston and Marcus Threston.

Charles Virtue, John Dougherty.
District No. 3—Samuel Houseman, George Harnet, Walter Harter.
District No. 4—John F. Groat, Thos. McCarthy, Louis Glushefski, James Dougherty.
District No. 5—Gershon B. Lamereaux.
District No. 6—Michael Gillespie, Martin Curley, John Threston, William Driscoll.
Every man who is twenty-one years old and not yet thirty-one must register, no matter what may be his physical conditions. Aliens are also subject to call and must register.

**THESE MEN WILL TAKE THE NAMES OF CONSCRIPT SOLDIERS.**

The following have been named to enroll our male residents subject to military duty on June 5.
First ward—Thomas J. Reese, Oswald Moore, Frank Marts, Frank Grob-

fires. But this m about a carnival to ough.

In reading the pa very important coi young people are l carnival tents and I rounds them. If i in towns that are be true here wh ground is near the was one case of taken away with a I heard of two case and boys into bad courts.

Our police and fi the carnival groun see that no young at large. Let us at the carnival wit behind it after it I

LOCAL BOYS F

News clipping source: Wilkes - Barre Sunday Independent 1917-05-27

# John J. Threston
# elected Justice of the Peace
# in 1902 at age 30

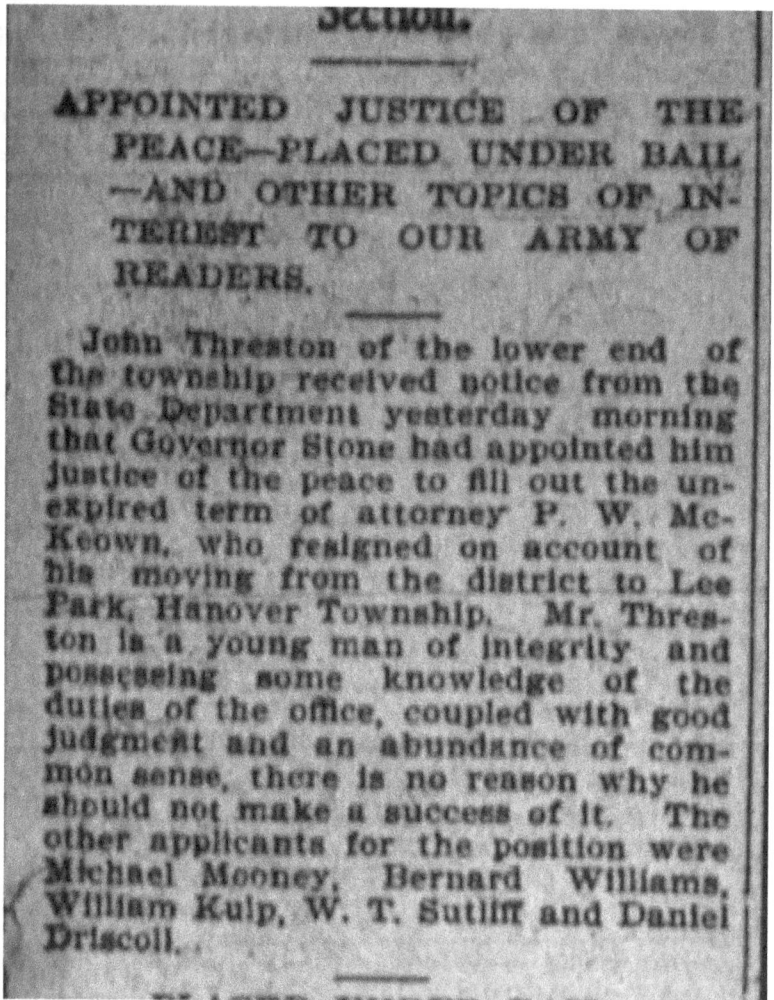

Section.

APPOINTED JUSTICE OF THE PEACE—PLACED UNDER BAIL —AND OTHER TOPICS OF INTEREST TO OUR ARMY OF READERS.

John Threston of the lower end of the township received notice from the State Department yesterday morning that Governor Stone had appointed him justice of the peace to fill out the unexpired term of attorney P. W. McKeown, who resigned on account of his moving from the district to Lee Park, Hanover Township. Mr. Threston is a young man of integrity and possessing some knowledge of the duties of the office, coupled with good judgment and an abundance of common sense, there is no reason why he should not make a success of it. The other applicants for the position were Michael Mooney, Bernard Williams, William Kulp, W. T. Sutliff and Daniel Driscoll.

News clipping source: The Wilkes-Barre Record, 30 Jul 1902, Wed, Page 11

# John J. Threston
# elected Town Auditor
# in 1902 at age 30

of the Fourth ward, which was left there for safe keeping. The ballots were taken out and scattered all about the floor. The gang which perpetrated this outrage was no doubt in search of the box of some other ward where the contest was close, with the intention of putting in a few substitutes and then entering a contest.

John Threston and William Driscoll, the Democratic candidates for auditor in the township, were elected by a fair sized majority.

The next council will be composed of S. L. French, George Hooven, Hugh Jones, John F. Connole, Job D. Powell, Eugene Bonham, Frank Moss, John Barton, William Walters, W. A. Loughrey, J. Lewis, D. W. Reese and Samuel Kendig.

The vote for school director in the Tenth ward was 55 each, and not 51,

News clipping source: The Wilkes-Barre Record (Wilkes-Barre, Pennsylvania)
20 Feb 1902, Thu • Page 8

The following are various news clippings (some are repeats) that mention John J. Threston. Each has been documented and sourced so no argument or dispute can be further brought about questioning whether or not John J. Threston was historically significant to the town of Plymouth, Pennsylvania. He absolutely was a very important part of the town's history.


**Occupations of John J. Thresten**

- **Justice of the Peace**
- **Auditor for Plymouth Township (Pennsylvania)**
- **Truant Officer for Plymouth Township (Pennsylvania)**

**Election results 1908 for Plymouth, PA - John Threston elected**
Source  The Wilkes-Barre Record (Wilkes-Barre, Pennsylvania) 19 Feb 1908, Wed • Page 13

## Justice of the Peace

Date: Saturday, April 25, 1908
Location: Wilkes-barre, Pennsylvania
Paper: *Wilkes-Barre Times-Leader*
Article type: Newspaper Article

J. W. Bogert, Twelfth ward, city.
B. F. Marshall, Sixth ward, city.
Michael E. Gaughan, Second ward, city.
John Threston, Plymouth township.
James Schultz, Fifth ward, Pittston.
Hans Nelson, Parsons.
Jacob J. Zalawa, Newport.

## Justice of the Peace John Threston

Date: Saturday, February 21, 1903
Location: Wilkes-barre, Pennsylvania
Paper: *Wilkes-Barre Weekly Times*
Article type: Legal/Probate/Court

Moyer 672  As Five Forks will give a majority of no less than twelve for Allen and Lynn, their election is almost assured. John McDonugh was elected tax collector; Threston justice of the peace, Kennedy, treasurer, and Olachinski and Heidelberger, auditors.

Justice of the Peace John Threston
Source  The Wilkes-Barre Record (Wilkes-Barre, Pennsylvania) 30
Jul 1902, Wed • Page 11

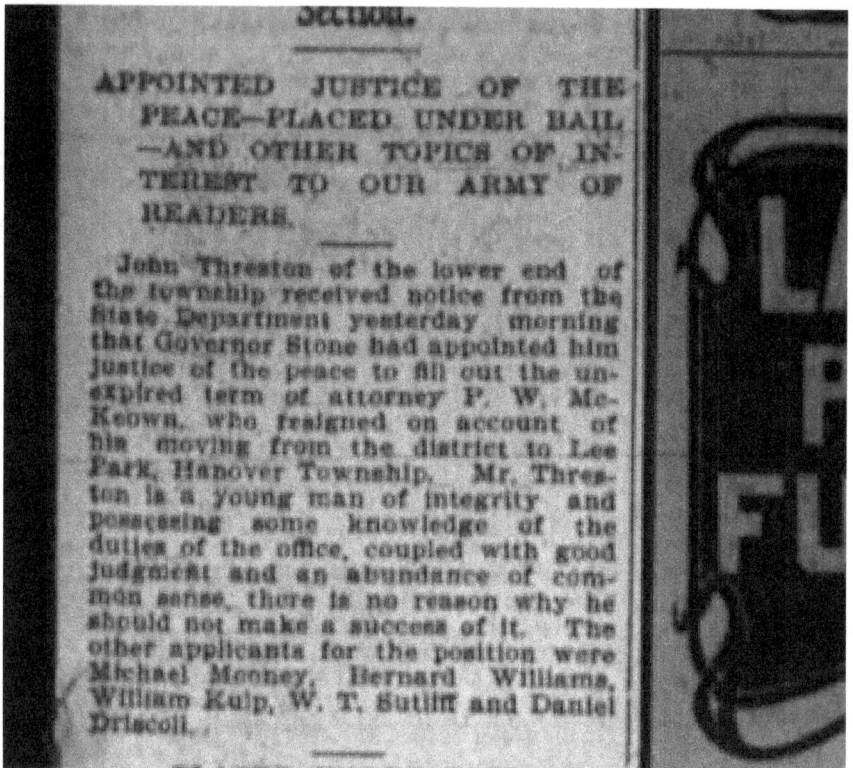

Section.

## APPOINTED JUSTICE OF THE PEACE—PLACED UNDER BAIL —AND OTHER TOPICS OF IN- TEREST TO OUR ARMY OF READERS.

John Threston of the lower end of the township received notice from the State Department yesterday morning that Governor Stone had appointed him justice of the peace to fill out the un- expired term of attorney P. W. Mc- Keown, who resigned on account of his moving from the district to Lee Park, Hanover Township. Mr. Thres- ton is a young man of integrity and possessing some knowledge of the duties of the office, coupled with good judgment and an abundance of com- mon sense, there is no reason why he should not make a success of it. The other applicants for the position were Michael Mooney, Bernard Williams, William Kulp, W. T. Sutliff and Daniel Driscoll.

Justice of the Peace John Threston
Source: The Wilkes-Barre Record (Wilkes-Barre, Pennsylvania)
10 Dec 1909, Fri • Page 21

## TOWNSHIP COMMISSIONERS MEET.

A meeting of the board of township commissioners was held at the usual time and place last evening. The meeting was called to order by president Curley and members William Burke and Wesley Allabaugh were present. Three of the members being residents of the upper end, now the borough of Larksville, two were appointed in their stead in the persons of Wiliam Mc-Geer and Michael McaCrthy, the other vacancy being left over until the next meeting. W. G. Allen, the well known merchant of West Nanticoke, was appointed treasurer and tax collector to fill the unexpired term of J. Carroll of the new borough. Township attorney John F. Boyle was instructed to proceed and adjust the indebtedness existing between the new borough and township. Prior to taking their chairs the two new members and the tax collector were sworn in by Justice of the peace John Threston.

Squire* John Thresten

Date: Tuesday, April 7, 1908
Location: Wilkes-barre, Pennsylvania
Paper: *Wilkes-Barre Times-Leader*
Article type: Newspaper Article

| Co., | witness fees in Monroe case, $46.20; | have a |
| $1.50; | Boston D. and II. mine, plank, $13.68; | keep hi |
| h Coal | Squire Threston, administering oaths, | Jame |
| , $7.50; | $3; Tague Shoolin for posts and rail- | who wa |
| Stoker, | ing, $7.50; Supervisor Derwin pay roll, | tive, in |
| George | $402.80; Robert Epstein, $8.70; Wil- | items h |

*Explanation of Squire (copied directly from Wikipedia)*

*"In the United States, this style is most common among attorneys, borrowing from the English tradition whereby all barristers were styled "esquires". (Solicitors were entitled only to the style "Mr".) In earlier years in the U.S., the title squire was given to a justice of the peace, for example Squire Jones. It was also used to mean justice of the peace as in the example, "He was taken before the squire." The connection to attorneys appears to have evolved from a time when squires meeting to negotiate a duel would instead resolve the dispute."*

# Auditor for Plymouth Township (Pennsylvania)

**ıouth.**

ıiness 180 f.

⸱⸱⸱⸱⸱⸱⸱⸱⸱⸱.$100,000

⸱⸱⸱⸱⸱⸱⸱⸱⸱⸱.$175,000

RECTORS.

will perform their duties of the offices faithfully if elected to the offices to which they aspire. The township candidates selected were: For auditor, John Threston was nominated. For constables, Thomas Williams secured the Republican notmination and Michael Riley the Democratic. For

Date: Friday, May 26, 1905
Location: Wilkes-barre, Pennsylvania
Paper: *Wilkes-Barre Times*
Article type: Ad/Classified

JAMES KERRIGAN,
W. C. JOHNSON,
W. W. BROWN,
PATRICK McΓ⌐⌐⌐LD,
JOHN THRESTON,
P. H. GAVIN,
                    Board of Auditors.

**Auditor for Plymouth Township (Pennsylvania)**

Source: The Wilkes-Barre Record (Wilkes-Barre, Pennsylvania)
20 Feb 1902, Thu • Page 8

of the Fourth ward, which was left there for safe keeping. The ballots were taken out and scattered all about the floor. The gang which perpetrated this outrage was no doubt in search of the box of some other ward where the contest was close, with the intention of putting in a few substitutes and then entering a contest.

John Threston and William Driscoll, the Democratic candidates for auditor in the township, were elected by a fair sized majority.

The next council will be composed of S. L. French, George Hooven, Hugh Jones, John F. Connole, Job D. Powell, Eugene Bonham, Frank Moss, John Barton, William Walters, W. A. Loughrey, J. Lewis, D. W. Reese and Samuel Kendig.

The vote for school director in the Tenth ward was 55 each, and not 51,

**John Threston served as Military Enrollment Officer for Plymouth, PA**

**Source: Wilkes-Barre Sunday Independent  1917-05-27**

Charles Virtue, John Dougherty.

District No. 3—Samuel Houseman, George Harnet, Walter Harter.

District No. 4—John F. Groat, Thos. McCarthy, Louis Glushefski, James Dougherty.

District No. 5—Gershon B. Lamereaux.

District No. 6—Michael Gillespie, Martin Curley, John Threston, William Driscoll.

Every man who is twenty-one years old and not yet thirty-one must register, no matter what may be his physical conditions. Aliens are also subject to call and must register.

## THESE MEN WILL TAKE THE NAMES OF CONSCRIPT SOLDIERS.

The following have been named to enroll our male residents subject to military duty on June 5.

First ward—Thomas J. Reese, Oswald Moore, Frank Marts, Frank Grob-

fires. But this n
about a carnival to
ough.

In reading the pa
very important coi
young people are 1
carnival tents and l
rounds them. If a
in towns that are
be true here wh
ground is near the c
was one case of
taken away with a
I heard of two case
and boys into bad
courts.

Our police and fi
the carnival ground
see that no young
at large. Let us s
at the carnival wil
behind it after it I

LOCAL BOYS F

# George McLean v. Charles C. Bowman

*It should be noted and included that when John J. Threston was presented to Wikipedia for inclusion, the original inclusion was revoked (and John J. Threston deleted) due to the argument that this case did not exist and/or the importance of the case. It is stated for the record that the McLean vs Bowman case was indeed real and can be found in newspapers such as The Wilkes Barre Record and, books as well as government records, specifically Records of the U.S. House of Representatives RG.233.62.House 62nd Congress Finding aid prepared by Office of Art and Archives, Office of the Clerk, U.S. House of Representatives.*

*Once again showing that Wikipedia is not always accurate or correct even though often cited. It is a shame that Wikipedia is operated by non-historians and others without knowledge and allowed to govern what is included. This decision also effected other inclusions that also have historical significance such as Sir Edward Threston who is a documented Knights Templar. Additionally it should be noted for the record that this is not "sour grapes" on part of the researchers or the Threston family.*

*Other far more high profile individuals such as professional golfer Fuzzy Zoeller had defamatory remarks made about him in Wikipedia, and, John Seigenthaler suffered character assassination on Wikipedia thus proving the point Wikipedia is hardly a true source of honest, correct and real information.*

*The information provided has been researched and documented in a way that all sources are made publicly available with the hope that one day the Threston family will take their rightful place in true historical records and accounting that are fact based.*

*In the meantime the good people of the Plymouth*
*(Pennsylvania) Historical Society have graciously accepted*
*the information provided on this website and have*
*expressed their appreciation of the information and*
*documentations found here. They will add the information*
*to their records and database in due time.*

McLEAN VS. BOWMAN. 365

Mr. JENKINS. Isn't it a fact, Mr. Campbell, that Judge Fuller in this court
in a primary contest departed from the practice that you have——
(It is agreed between counsel that Jonathan R. Davis will be called at 2
o'clock, Monday afternoon. Adjourned until 9 a. m., Monday, Mar. 20, 1911.)

*NOTICE OF HEARING, NAMES OF WITNESSES, ETC.*

To Hon. CHARLES C. BOWMAN, contestee, or Hon. FRANK W. WHEATON and
EVAN C. JONES, Esq., his attorneys:
You are hereby notified that on Monday, the 20th day of March, 1911, at 9
o'clock in the forenoon, at the office of W. S. McLean, Esq., No. 713 Coal
Exchange Building, Wilkes-Barre, Pa., and at such other times and places to
which adjournments may be taken and such other witnesses as may be here-
after subpœnaed and notice of their production given to you, before Arthur L.
Turner, a notary public of the State of Pennsylvania, residing in the city of
Wilkes-Barre, in said county, duly commissioned and acting as such, and hereby
designated as an officer for issuing writs of subpœnas and requiring the
attendance of witnesses before him, as provided by sections 109, 110, and 111,
of the Revised Statutes of the United States, depositions will be taken of
witnesses whose names and places of residence are as follows:
Michael Cavanaugh, Ashley, Pa.; Thomas Poynton, Swoyersville, Pa.; Thomas
Roche, Swoyersville, Pa.; John Laverick, Swoyersville, Pa.; Harry Miller,
Swoyersville, Pa.; Jacob Miller, Swoyersville, Pa.; John Lore, Plymouth
Township, Pa.; William McGeer, Plymouth Township, Pa.; William Sanders,
Plymouth Township, Pa.; Michael Gillespie, Plymouth Township, Pa.; John
Davis, Plymouth Township, Pa.; John Thresten, Plymouth Township, Pa.;
Martin Curley, Plymouth Township, Pa.; Edward Quinn, Plymouth Township,
Pa.; Geary A. Dills, Duryea, Pa.; Arthur E. Price, Duryea, Pa.; Thomas
O'Boyle, Duryea, Pa.; B. F. Griffith, Nanticoke, Pa.; William Chamberlain,
Nanticoke, Pa.; Isaac L. Edwards, Nanticoke, Pa.; James F. McFadden,
Edwardsville, Pa.; Thomas Devey, Wilkes-Barre, Pa.; Thomas Oliver, Wilkes-
Barre, Pa.; Crawford C. Smith, Wilkes-Barre, Pa.; Robert P. Robinson, Wilkes-
Barre, Pa.; Earl Crawford, Wilkes-Barre, Pa.; Robert Johnston, Wilkes-Barre,
Pa.; Samuel Griffiths, Ashley, Pa.; David Richards, Ashley, Pa.; Henry Bly,
Ashley, Pa.          •

GEO. R. McLEAN.

Service accepted this 17th day of March, 1911.

EVAN C. JONES,
*Attorney for Contestee.*

Service accepted March 17, 1911, as to Peter Gorham, Ashley, Pa., also.

EVAN C. JONES,
*Attorney for Contestee.*

*Reference ( ISBN-10: 1130574849 ISBN-13: 978-1130574845)*

The case as shown (below) in the book "A Historical and Legal Digest of All Contested Elections" by Merrill Moores that there was a question regarding expenses omitted totaling over $2000 and alternations were attempted to make the expenses appear legitimate. As elected Auditor of Plymouth, Pennsylvania, John Threston, would have been a very important witness to this case.

Contestee from the sworn return of expenses required by the Pennsylvania law omitted over $2,000 of his expenditures. He tried to conceal this excess by erasures and alterations on check stubs and memoranda. Much of this excess, if not all, was spent corruptly. Contestee unseated and seat left vacant.

McLean v. Bowman, 62d Cong_____p. 54

# Wife and Family of John J. Threston

- Margaret McLaughlin Smith 1875
- Married in December, 1895

John Threston Marriage

The Scranton Republican (Scranton, Pennsylvania) 25 December 1895 Page 8

at the Bloomingdale M. E. church, interment in Bloomingdale cemetery.

The following marriage licenses were
granted yesterday: William J. Lewis and
Marie Phillips, of Wilkes-Barre; A. P.
Harrison and Maggie E. Pritchard, of
Plymouth; Conrad Seiple, of Brown's Cor-
ners, Pa., and Stella Pringle, of Plymouth
township; John Threston, of Plymouth,
and Margaret Smith, of Edwardsville;
William H. Miller and Lena M. King, of
Pittston; John J. Griffin and Gretta Jones,
of Alden; George Maher and Augusta
Chamberlin, of Nanticoke; S. V. Mc-
Cracken and Sarah Wheeler, of Wilkes-
Barre; William H. Knittle and Laura
Smith, of Wilkes-Barre.

## Children

- Leonard Threston (approximately 1896 to November, 1903 (died at age 7, see news clipping below)+
- John Thresten 1898 (Died in childhood)
- Margaret Threston 1903 – 1987
- Evelyn Thresten-Zoransky 1905 – 1976
- Marie Threston 1907 – 1983
- Joseph Threston 1909 – 1994
- Gerald Threston 1910 (Died in childhood)
- Leonard Marcus Threston 1912 – 1999+
- Vincent Threston 1914 – 1982

+It should be noted that John J. Threston and Margaret McLaughlin Threston had two sons named Leonard. The first died at the age of 7 in November, 1903 and was born approximately 1896. The clipping below shows the evidence of this new information.

Source: The Wilkes-Barre Record (Wilkes-Barre, Pennsylvania) 6 Nov 1903, Fri • Page 13

from the bat of one of the men. The injured men are William Burdulis and Dominick Masanis and their two laborers. The men named were the more seriously burned of the four and were taken to their homes in the ambulance. The others were able to walk home.

### FUNERALS YESTERDAY.

Yesterday afternoon occurred the funeral of Leonard, the 7-year-old son of Mr. and Mrs. John Threston of Curry Hill. The cortege was a long one, many friends of the family attending. Interment was in St. Vincent's Cemetery.

James McCloskey, the young man who died at Mercy Hospital on Tuesday from the effects of inhaling sulphurous fumes, took place yesterday afternoon from the home of his aunt. Services were conducted at St. Vincent's Church by Rev. D. W. McCarthy in the pres-

**John and Margaret Threston Children and their occupations and spouses**

- Leonard Threston (approximately 1896 to November, 1903)
- John Thresten 1898 (Died in childhood)
- Margaret Threston 1903 – 1987  - never married, teacher
- Evelyn Threston-Zoransky 1905 – 1976 married Joseph C. Zoransky
- Marie Threston 1907 – 1983  never married, clerical worker
- Joseph Threston 1909 – 1994  married Esther Rindgen
- Gerald Threston 1910 (Died in childhood)
- Leonard Marcus Threston 1912 – 1999  married Mary T. Harnen
- Vincent Threston 1914 – 1982 married Dorothy

# Death

It should be noted John J. Thresten was titled as Gentleman at the time of death. This is the strongest "modern day" evidence of the Thresten/Threston family nobility ties that date back for centuries.

| | |
|---|---|
| Name: | Mr John Threston (Title: Gentleman) |
| Gender: | Male |
| Race: | White |
| Age: | 64 |
| Birth Date: | 13 Nov 1874 |
| Birth Place: | Plymouth, Pennsylvania |
| Death Date: | 24 Sep 1939 |
| Death Place: | Wilkes-Barre, Luzerne, Pennsylvania, USA |
| Father Name: | Richard Threston |
| Father Birth Place: | England |
| Mother Name: | Veronica Burke |
| Mother Birth Place: | England |
| Spouse Name: | Mary Mclaughlin Threston |
| Certificate Number: | 82271 |

**Title of Gentleman (copied directly from Wikipedia as a source of reference and explanation.)**

In its original meaning, the term denoted a man of the lowest rank of the English gentry, standing below an esquire and above a yeoman. By definition, this category included the younger sons of the younger sons of peers and the younger sons of baronets (after this honour's institution in 1611), knights, and esquires in perpetual succession, and thus the term captures the common denominator of gentility (and often armigerousness) shared by both constituents of the English aristocracy: the peerage and the gentry. In this sense, the word equates with the French *gentilhomme* ("nobleman"), which latter term has been, in Great Britain, long confined to the peerage; Maurice Keen points to the category of "gentlemen" in this context as thus constituting "the nearest contemporary English equivalent of the *noblesse* of France" (*Origins of the English Gentleman*, 2002, p. 9).

# Copy of Death Certificate – John J. Threston

## Sources

1. Pennsylvania Historical and Museum Commission
2. Original data: Pennsylvania (State). Death certificates, 1906–1963. Series 11.90 (1,905 cartons). Records of the Pennsylvania Department of Health, Record Group 11. Pennsylvania Historical and Museum Commission, Harrisburg, Pennsylvania. Record 82271.

# Margaret Threston Rutledge

We know very little about Margaret Threston Rutledge other than she was sibling to John J. Threston, and, that she was the wife of Robert C. Rutledge, Bakery Owner in Wilkes Barre, PA. Rutledge was son of Robert Rutledge (Born in Bellina, County Mayo, Ireland. He came to the U.S. in 1844) and Anna O'Hearn. The Threston family also lived in County Mayo, Ireland where they were part of the land gentry.

There is no record of children, however, we do know that she died young.

# Patrick Threston

Patrick Threston was the only (known) Threston to stay in New York City. Records indicated that Partick and his wife Bridget lived in both Manhattan and Brooklyn.

# Ellen Threston

Ellen Threston is the least known, and, very little information is available. We only know she was born in November in England and died in Plymouth, Pennsylvania.

# Peter Threston Family

Far less is known about Peter Threston, brother of John J. Threston, however, the following information and clippings were found during the research of this book. Peter Threston was born in England, and, immigrated to the United States in the late 1800s.

He married Mary Bryan, an orphan, and, together they had five children, most notably Marcus Threston, who would later go on to form and lead The Threston Orchestra.

Children of Peter Threston and Mary Bryan

- **Richard George Threston    1890 – 1970**
- **Terrance Threston    1893 – ?**
- **Winifred Threston Coughlin    1896 - ?**
  - *note: Winifred Threston married William J. Coughlin son of William Coughlin and Bridget Grout (1867 – 1908)*
- **Marcus Threston    1898 – ?**
- **Cecillia Threston 1900 - 1901 died of pneumonia at age 4 months**

# Marriage Certificate of Peter Threston and Mary Bryan

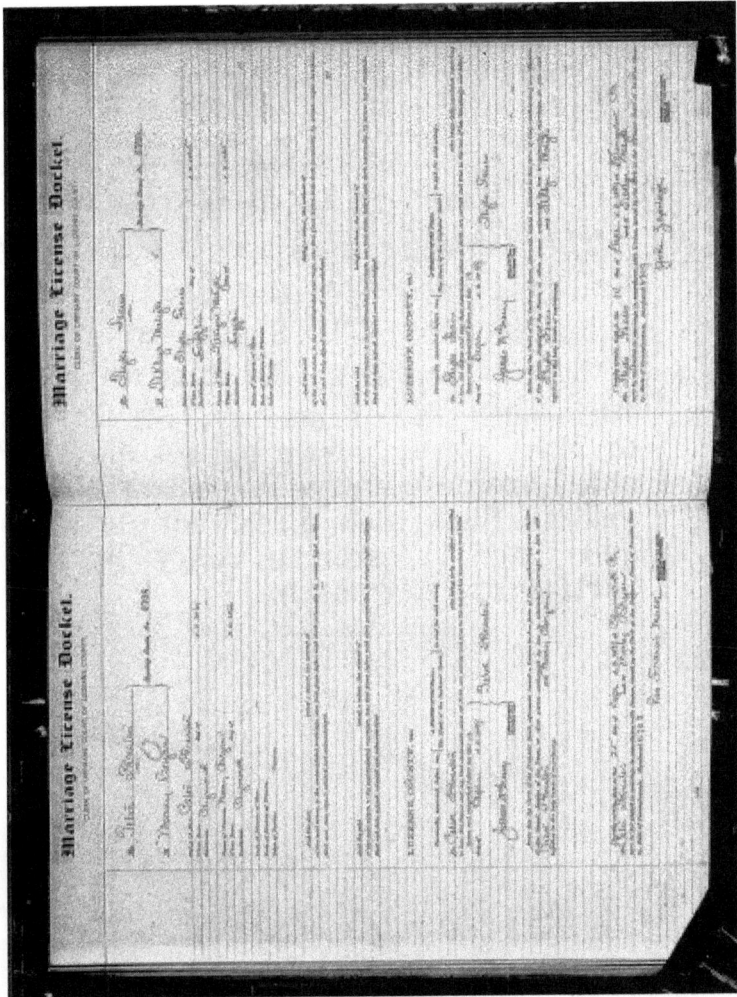

**Transcription of text**

Name: Peter Thresten

Event Type: Marriage

Event Date: 25 Sep 1889

Event Place: , Luzerne, Pennsylvania, United States

Spouse's Name: Mary Bryan

Reference ID: 6708 , GS Film Number: 955879 , Digital Folder Number: 004268745 , Image Number: 00584

Peter Threston and Mary Bryan Wedding Announcement

Source: The Scranton Republican, 14 Sep 1889, Sat, Page 6

### Marriage Licenses Granted.

The following marriage licenses were yesterday granted by the Register of Wills: John Chase to Ella Smith, both parties of Wilkes-Barre; John Rugintz to Mary Hlawith, both also of this city; Steven Wackata to Mary Surgent, both parties of Mt. Pleasant, Luzerne county; P. Gritz, of Hazleton, to Loise Slein, also a resident of that place; and Peter Threston to Mary Bryan, both parties from Plymouth.

# 25th Wedding Anniversary for Peter and Mary Threston

Source: **Wilkes-Barre Semi-Weekly Record**

Wilkes-Barre, Pennsylvania
Tue, Sep 29, 1914 – Page 5

Mr. and Mrs. Peter Threston of Cherry street, residents of this place since childhood, celebrated the twenty-fifth or silver anniversary of their marriage at the family home last evening. The couple were married at St. Vincent's Church Sept. 25, 1889, by the late Rev. T. J. Donahoe. They have resided here continuously since and the lapse of years has but endeared them to all who have the pleasure of their acquaintance. Music was furnished by orchestra composed of Benjamin Harris, oJhn Coper and Marcus Threston. A program of vocal and instrumental music was also provided and a five-course dinner served. Among those present were Mrs. William Craig, Mr. and Mrs. Michael Kennedy, Mr. and Mrs. Thomas Bresnahan, Mr. and Mrs. John Lynch, Mr. and Mrs. Michael Eiserlo, Mr. and Mrs. John Threston and family, Mr. and Mrs. Daniel Bryan and family, Mrs. Thomas Walker and family, Mr. and Mrs. James Brennan, Mr. and Mrs. George Detmore, Mr. and Mrs. Dominick Mangan, Mr. and Mrs. William Bryan, Mrs. P. Tracy and family, Mr. and Mrs. J. Connell and family, Mr. and Mrs. John Burke and family, Mr. and Mrs. W. B. Cleary, Misses Frances Girton, Ellen Threston, Winifred Threston, Mary Lynch, Annie Lynch, Mary Burke, B. Burke, Margaret Lynch, Mary C. Lynch, Mary Bryant, Margaret Tracy, Clara Corr d, Nellie Bryan, Carrie Clifton, Nellie Reed, Katie Dougherty, Sue Dough rty, Katie Coughlin, Nellie Detmore, Mary Detmore, Mary Tracy, Regina Walker and Josephine Craig, Richard Threston, Terrance Threston, Harry Wing, John Cooper, Jeff Nowatnick, Michael Bryan and Edward Bryan.
[Correspondence, Sept. 28.]

Lady's Aux. Ancient Order of Hibernians lawn party hosted at the home of Peter Threston, Willow St. Plymouth PA
The Wilkes-Barre Record, 11 Jul 1918, Thu, Page 17

A whirlwind of action, dramatic escapes, desperate battle and big love story. Also Sunshine comedy, "Are Married Policemen Safe?" Matinee, 5c.

---

Miss Mary Beacham of Buttonwood, entertained Miss Betty Lloyd and Henry Gehring of Utica, N. Y., over the week end.

Ladies' Auxiliary, Division No. 7, Ancient Order of Hibernians, will give a social on the lawn at the home of P. Threston, Willow street, July 15.

The funeral of Joseph Brozena, of Templeton's alley will be held this afternoon at 2:30 o'clock with services at St. Mary's Nativity Church and interment in St. Mary's Cemetery.

Edward Condron, a native and well known young man of this place but for the next few years of Detroit

**Peter Threston Juror (Lackawanna Bridge Company negligence case)**
Source: The Wilkes-Barre Record, 22 Jun 1917, Fri, Page 18

Dr. Groblewski, who examined deceased, John Lewis and Ray Davis, laborers for the Buffalo concern.

The jury rendered a verdict to the effect that "William McDermott, came to his death from an electrical shock and we find the Lackawanna Bridge Company negligent in not providing a safe place for the receased to work by protecting him from underlying high tension wires." The jurors were: Peter Threston, William Davis, Joseph James, Max Gerstein, David Reese and John Johnson.

**Peter Threston hit by train**

**Source The Wilkes-Barre Record, 7 Aug 1919, Thu, Page 18**

### Train Hits Threston

Peter Threston, of Willow street, a lifelong resident of Plymouth while walking along the Lackawanna railroad Tuesday night was hit by the locomotive of an east bound freight and thrown some distance. Fortunately a couple members of the crew were sitting on the pilot and seeing Mr. Threston in the distance signaled the engineer who applied the brakes, reversed the lever, and blew the whistle but the train was upon him before he could get out of the way with the result that he was considerably bruised about the body and cut on the face. Coming to a stop the crew picked up Mr. Threston, and he was later taken to his home and medical aid summoned.

The accident occurred at a point near the power plant of Luzerne County Gas & Electric Co. and it is fortunate for him that he was seen in time otherwise he would without doubt be crushed to death under the wheels.

# Marcus Threston and the Threston Orchestra

Marcus Threston was the son of Peter and Mary Threston, and, a very accomplished musician. He began his career in childhood, and, lead his own orchestra and was part of the 42nd Infantry Band at Fort Slocum, New York during World War I in July, 1918. He died just a few short months later at the age of 20 of pneumonia. The orchestra continued without Marcus until 1919/1920 but appears to have discontinued at that point.

a former assistant at St. Vincent's Church, but now of St. Mary's Church, Wilkes-Barre.

Wanted—A driver for Fire Co. No. 1. Apply W. P. Yaple.

Marcus Threston, son of Mr. and Mrs. Threston, of Willow street, having enlisted, will leave Saturday to join the 42nd Infantry Band at Fort Slocum, N. Y. Mr. Threston is a qualified musician, he being leader for some time past of Threston's orchestra.

At the Hippodrome To-day William Fox presents Jewel Carmen in "Confession," in six acts. Also two real Sunshine comedy, "My Wife's Husband." Special matinee, 5c.

News clipping source: The Wilkes-Barre Record (Wilkes-Barre, Pennsylvania)
25 July 1918, Thu • Page 17

street in front of hall, right resting on

## Sodalis Club Dance

State Armory, Plymouth

### THURSDAY EVENING

**Music by Threston's Orchestra**

This is the last dance of the season. Come and have a good time.

Newsclipping Source: The Wilkes-Barre Record
Wilkes-Barre, Pennsylvania
Thu, May 29, 1919 – Page 26

KOVAC—At Midvale, Nov. 6, 1918, Joh
Kovac, aged 40, of influenza.

GRINKAVICZ—At Georgetown, Nov.
1918, Matthew Grinkavicz, aged 46,
pneumonia.

STEFAN—In City Hospital, Nov. 7, 191
Mrs. Katherine Stefan, aged 26, of bron
chial pneumonia.

PATRICIA—In Wilkes-Barre, Nov. 7, 191
Sister Mary, Patricia, of influenza.

THRESTON—At Plymouth, Nov. 7, 191
Marcus Threston, aged 20, of pneumoni

BOLTHRUSES—At Larksville, Nov.
1918, William Bolthruses, aged 24,
pneumonia.

JANOV—In Wilkes-Barre, Nov. 6, 191
Mrs. Eva Janov, aged 27, of pneumoni

McMANAMNO—In France, 1918, Dani
McManamon of Sugar Notch.

HOBAN—At San Francisco, Nov. 3, 191
Mrs. Frank Hoban, formerly of Wilke
Barre, of influenza.

News clipping source:  The Wilkes-Barre Record, 8 Nov 1918, Fri, Page 20

# Baseball Team (Threston)

The Threstons appeared to have a baseball team in the early 1900s.
It appears to have been a company team. The following newspaper
clipping support this claim.

to-morrow on account of the Jewisl
New Year.
  All members of the Epworth Leagu
are requested to' meet with .W  J
Hooper this evening at the close  o
prayer meeting.
  Harry Oppenheimer will close  hi
place of business to-day on account ·o
holiday.
  Kearney's and Threston's base bal
teams will play a game at Washingor
Park Sunday afternoon.
  The Spring Brook Water Supply Co
has started the work of laying  th
thirty-six-inch mains from the connec
tion at the river to the tunnel in th
mountain. A large force of hands i
taking out the dirt on Coal street an·
yesterday the pipes were laid unde
the Lackawanna Railroad tracks.
  A business meeting of the Men'

Source: The Wilkes-Barre Record, 2 Oct 1913, Thu, Page 19

absent four weeks, but will make a couple of visits home in the meantime.

For Sale—Will sell at a bargain. Square piano, dining room table, two desks and bedstead. Apply 150 Church street.

Threston and Kearney's base ball aggregation and East Plymouth and Nationals will play base ball to-morrow afternoon; the former at the Washington field and the latter at Lowertown Park.

Top Coats, a large variety. Prices from $10, $12, $15 to $25. Look them over. Harry Oppenheimer.

Mrs. W. C. Stiff left at noon yesterday to spend a few days in New York, from where she will go to Asbury

Source: The Wilkes-Barre Record, 4 Oct 1913, Sat, Page 25

# Miscellaneous News Clippings

**Plymouth All Stars Football Team (Player: F. Threston)**

Source:  The Wilkes-Barre Record (Wilkes-Barre, Pennsylvania) 6 Nov 1915, Sat • Page 9

## Lee Park to Play Plymouth

The Lee Park A. A. foot ball eleven, which so far has won every game played, are finally to meet the Plymouth All Stars, composed mainly of former Welsh Hill players, on the Breslau gridiron on Sunday. Plymouth team will use the following line up: A. Evans, G. Davis, H. Hughes, H. Thomas, D. Hughes, C. Reese, A. Cooper, A. Floyd, F. Threston, E. Young, J. Horsefield, B. Jones, B. Brennan, C. Rilk, Strojny, K. Frederick and J. Shovlin.

Manager Bender of Lee Park wants the following players to report Sunday at 10 o'clock for practice: J. Bender, B. Jenkins, MsAnneny, Hanagan, Coxe, Reckus, Ryan, W. Williams, Dryer, Marvin, Bryant, Telepszo, S. Williams, Smith, D. Morris, D. Williams and Roman.

The game will start at 3:30.

**Threston Cigar Store, West Main Street, Plymouth, PA**

Source:  **The Wilkes-Barre Record, 14 Dec 1912, Sat, Page 32**

our great sale, 50c blue serge pull-down caps at 25c.  Sale ends Saturday night.  Harry Oppenheimer, successor to D. Kabatchnick.

Frank J. Kline will take possession of his new cigar store and pool parlors this morning.

The contest for the benefit of John Gillespie, who through an accident a few months ago had to have an arm amputated, will be decided this evening at Threston's cigar store, West Main street.

The funeral of Mrs. Evan Rees, of Eno street, who was found dead in

**O'Brien and Threston Cigar Store and Pool Parlor**
Source: **The Wilkes-Barre Record, 16 Jul 1914, Thu, Page 19**

O'Brien & Threston, conductors of a pool parlor and cigar store at Bull Run Crossing on Main street, have dissolved partnership, the former retiring. The latter will continue the business as heretofore.

Miss Mary Costello of Gardner street left yesterday for Philadelphia to follow her profession, that of trained nurse at Hahnemann Homeopathic Hospital. Her sister, Miss Nellie, who is also a trained nurse, went to Baltimore.

**Patrick Threston pall bearer at Kreig funeral March 1914**

Source:  The Wilkes-Barre Record (Wilkes-Barre, Pennsylvania)
30 Mar 1914, Mon • Page 23

## Funerals of a Day

Saturday morning occurred the funeral of William Kreig from his late home, Cherry street, to St. Vincent's Church, where Rev. T. M. Jordan read the requiem mass at 9:30 o'clock. Many out of town friends of the departed were present at the obsequies, and numerous floral offerings testified to the affection in which deceased was held. The flower carriers were Arthur Glidden, John Farrell, Dionysius Walsh and John Morrissey; pall bearers, Joseph Gaynor, Patrick Threston, George Detmore, William Dailey, Patrick Gaynor and Patrick Tracey. Interment was in St. Vincent's Cemetery.

John J. Threston Hunting Trip 1909
Source: The Wilkes-Barre Record (Wilkes-Barre, Pennsylvania) 5
Oct 1909, Tue • Page 17

The boys and young men of the Pilgrim Congregational Church clubbed together and purchased a new and handsome bible, which was presented to the pastor on Sunday morning.

---

I like Hartman's soda, but, Oh, you root beer.

---

Justice of the peace John Threston of the west end of the township has returned from a successful hunting trip.

Miss Nellie, daughter of Mr. and Mrs. George A. Bound, has returned from an extended visit to friends in New York City, Boston, Springfield, and Westfield, Mass.

Thomas Granahan has returned from New York, where he went to see the sights of the Hudson-Fulton cele-

**Other Threston sports/baseball related news clipping**

**The Crawfords, Luzerne County baseball Champs 1905**
**Threston, team captian**

**Source:  The Wilkes-Barre Record, 18 Jul 1905, Tue, Page 13**

the batting of the Shamrocks who batter two pitchers out of the box.

---

The Shamrocks of Plains will play the Willows from Sebastopol on July 24. Answer through the Record.

---

The Crawfords of Plymouth challenge the Royal Blues or the Sans Souci on July 23, on the Crawfords' diamond. The Crawfords have won nine games and have not been defeated and now claim the championship of Luzerne County. Answer through the Record, or call up new 'phone 7167 Threston, captain; Lynch, manager.

---

The Crawfords defeated the Welsh Hill Tigers by a score of 16 to 4. The batteries—Crawfords, Tracy and Mc-Monigle; Tigers, Bruce and Barrett.

---

The Brookside Stars would like to

## Official Register of the United States ... - Volume 1 - Page 710 (Patrick Threston, Brooklyn, NY)

---

## Threston - Connell Marriage on August 28, 1912 in Plymouth, PA

### Source: The Wilkes-Barre Record (Wilkes-Barre, Pennsylvania) 29 Aug 1912, Thu • Page 16

Kingston.

UREN—GREGORY—At Nanticoke. Aug. 28, 1912, by Rev. George A. Warburton, James Uren, Jr., of Nanticoke and Miss Myrtle Gregory of Hunlock Creek.

ANDREWS—DRUMMOND—At Pittston, Aug. 28, 1912, by Rev. Mr. Moore, Joseph Andrews and Miss Elizabeth Drummond, both of Pittston.

DRUMMOND—HOFFMAN—At Pittston, Aug. 28, 1912, by Rev. Mr. Rischke, Andrew Drummond and Miss Jennie Hoffman, both of Pittston.

JAMES—ALGER—At Avoca, Aug. 27, 1912, by Rev. James Moore, John James of Taylor and Miss Florence Alger of Avoca.

MOONEY—LIVINGSTON—At Nanticoke, Aug. 28, 1912, by Rev. J. V. Moylan, Henry A. Mooney of Wilkes-Barre and Miss Mary Livingston of Nanticoke.

BLAKE—CONNIFF—At Plymouth, Aug. 28, 1912, by Rev. T. M. Jordan, Patrick Blake and Mary Conniff, both of Plymouth Township.

CONNELL—THRESTON—At Plymouth, Aug. 28, 1912, by Rev. T. M. Jordan, James Connell of Plymouth and Veronica Threston of Plymouth Township.

WAGNER—JONES—At Lehman, Aug. 28, 1912, by Rev. J. R. Wagner, Harry J. Wagner and Mamie Jones, both of Plymouth.

### BIRTHS

To Mr. and Mrs. Charles Jones, Wilkes-Barre, Aug. 22, 1912, a daughter.

To Mr. and Mrs. William Loucks, Wilkes-Barre, Aug. 25, 1912, a daughter.

To Mr. and Mrs. James D. Smith, Wilkes-Barre, Aug. 25, 1912, a daughter.

**Mary (Margaret)Threston wife of John J. Threston, Justice of the Peace has surgery**

Source: The Wilkes-Barre Record (Wilkes-Barre, Pennsylvania) 20 Jun 1910, Mon • Page 17

to their summer home at Clanco, N. J., where they will reside until early fall when they will take up their residence in Philadelphia.

## SHORT NOTES AND PERSONALS.

Michael J. Feeney, Morgan Lewis, J. C. Lewis, Case Todd and John J. Maher will do jury duty this week.

Mrs. John Threston, wife of John Threston, justice of the peace of the township, underwent another operation at the Mercy Hospital Thursday; and was reported last evening as improving nicely.

## ARE YOU GOING TO EUROPE?

We are agents for the White Star, Cunard, Anchor, American and all the other steamship lines, and have arranged many attractive summer ex-

# Threston and Spencer and Churchill Ahnentafel

It has taken over four years of research to prove the Threston family ties to the Churchill (including Sir Winston Churchill) and Spencer (including Princess Diana) but are in fact blood relatives. (The evidence is indisputable.)

## Ahnentafel, Generation No. 1 - Gentleman John J. Threston

John J. Threston was born 13 Nov 1872 in Plymouth, Luzerne, Pennsylvania, USA, and died 24 Sep 1939 in Wilkes-Barre, Luzerne, Pennsylvania, USA. He was the son of 2. Richard Treston and 3. Veronica Burke Threston. He married Mary (Margaret) McLaughlin Threston 1896, daughter of McLaughlin. She was born 4 October 1873 in Wilkes-Barre, Pennsylvania, USA, and died in Wilkes Barre, Luzerne, Pennsylvania, United States of America.

## Ahnentafel, Generation No. 2

Richard Treston was born 1830 in ireland, and died 1868 in Pennsylvania, United States. He was the son of 4. Richard Treston MD and 5. Hannah Treston. 3.   Veronica Burke Threston. She was the daughter of 6. Burke.          Children of Veronica Burke Threston and Richard Treston are:    i.    Peter Threston was born Jun 1861 in England, and died in Plymouth, Luzerne, Pennsylvania, United States. He married Mary Bryan - Threston 1890. She was born Jan 1866 in Pennsylvania. He married Mary Threston 1890, daughter of Patrick Threston and Bridget. She was born Jan 1866 in Pennsylvania. He married Mary 1890. She was born Jan 1866 in Pennsylvania, United States.        ii.    Ellen Thresten was born Nov 1863 in England, and died in Plymouth, Luzerne, Pennsylvania, United States.      iii.    Margaret Thresten - Rutledge was born abt 1867 in England. She married Robert C. Rutledge 29 Jul 1898 in Luzerne, Pennsylvania. He was born Nov 1866 in Pennsylvania. 1.    iv.    John J. Threston was born 13 Nov

1872 in Plymouth, Luzerne, Pennsylvania, USA, and died 24 Sep 1939 in Wilkes-Barre, Luzerne, Pennsylvania, USA. He married Mary (Margaret) McLaughlin Threston 1896, daughter of McLaughlin. She was born 4 October 1873 in Wilkes-Barre, Pennsylvania, USA, and died in Wilkes Barre, Luzerne, Pennsylvania, United States of America.     v.    Ellen Threston was born in England.     vi.    Mary.

## Ahnentafel, Generation No. 3

Richard Treston MD was born about 1791 in Tulrahan, Ireland, and died 1864 in Roscommon, Mayo, Ireland. He was the son of 8. Luke Treston and 9. Ann OConnor-Treston.  5.    Hannah Treston was born about 1791 in Norfolk, England.          Child of Hannah Treston and Richard Treston MD is: 2.    i.    Richard Treston was born 1830 in ireland, and died 1868 in Pennsylvania, United States. He married Veronica Burke Threston, daughter of Burke.  6. Burke.          Child of Burke is: 3.    i.    Veronica Burke Threston. She married Richard Treston, son of Richard Treston MD and Hannah Treston. He was born 1830 in ireland, and died 1868 in Pennsylvania, United States.

## Ahnentafel, Generation No. 4

Luke Treston was born 1764 in Tulrahan, Ireland. He was the son of 16. John Treston.  9.    Ann OConnor-Treston was born 1764 in Ireland, and died 1846 in County, Mayo, Ireland.          Children of Ann OConnor-Treston and Luke Treston are:    i.    John Treston was born 1789 in Tulrahan, Mayo, Ireland, and died 8 Oct 1864 in County, Mayo, Ireland. He married Catherine Cogan - Treston. She was born in Ireland. 4.    ii.    Richard Treston MD was born about 1791 in Tulrahan, Ireland, and died 1864 in Roscommon, Mayo, Ireland. He married Hannah Treston. She was born about 1791 in Norfolk, England.    iii.    Michael Treston was born 1794 in Tulrahan, Ireland.     iv.    Francis Treston was born 1796 in Tulrahan, Ireland.     v.    Patrick Treston was born

1798 in Tulrahan, Ireland. He married Julia Burk.      vi.   Luke
Treston was born 1802 in Tulrahan, Ireland, and died Dec 1879 in
Claremorris, Ireland.      vii.   Mary Ann Treston - Dillon was born
1806 in Tulrahan, Ireland. She married Edward Dillon. He was
born 1804 in Ireland.


## Ahnentafel, Generation No. 5

John Treston was born 1735 in Tulrahan, Ireland. He was the son
of 32. John Treston and 33. Mary Spencer.      Children of John
Treston are: 8.   i.   Luke Treston was born 1764 in Tulrahan,
Ireland. He married Ann OConnor-Treston. She was born 1764 in
Ireland, and died 1846 in County, Mayo, Ireland.      ii.   John
Treston was born 1767 in Ireland.      iii.   Catherine Treston.
iv.   Catherine Treston.


## Ahnentafel, Generation No. 6

John Treston. 33.   Mary Spencer. She was the daughter of 66.
John Robert Spencer and 67. Barbara Churchill.      Child of
Mary Spencer and John Treston is: 16.   i.   John Treston was
born 1735 in Tulrahan, Ireland.

# REFERENCES

Sources:

- FindMyPast.com
- Society of Genealogists
- http://eol.org (Encyclopedia of Life)
- Historical Research Center
- Board Certified Family Research
- Family Search

References and Sources

1. Devon Family History Society, PO Box 9, Exeter, EX2 6YP, UNITED KINGDOM
2. "A visitation of the seats and arms of the noblemen and gentlemen" by Sir John Bernard Burke- Page 62
3. "Notes and queries for Somerset and Dorset Volumes 5-6" by - Page 46
4. The Coventry leet book; or mayor's register: Issue 138; Issue 146 - Page 909
5. The Complete Peerage or a History of the House of Lords and All its Members From the Earliest Times, Volume XIV: Addenda & Corrigenda (Stroud, Gloucestershire, U.K.: Sutton Publishing, 1998),
6. A calendar of Norwich deeds enrolled in the court rolls of that city: years 1307-1341- Page 56
7. A short calendar of the deeds relating to Norwich - Page 56
8. The Bishop of London's Commissary Court 1578-1588 - Pages 113 and 287
9. The register of Henry Chichele, archbishop of Canterbury, 1414-1443: Volume 4
10. Canterbury and York Society: Volume 47
11. Index of Wills in the York Registry: 1554 to 1568 - Page 164

12. The Coventry Leet Book: or Mayor's register : Volume 1 - Page 180
13. Proceedings, Volume 8  By Suffolk Institute of Archaeology and History, Suffolk Institute of Archaeology - Page 363
14. The Coventry leet book,: Mayor's register: Issues 134-135
15. Leicestershire Archaeological and Historical Society, Leicestershire Architectural and Archaeological Society Transactions: Volume 23
16. Calendar of Inquisitions Post Mortem: Edward III
17. The place-names of Northumberland and Durham by Allen Mawer page 195
18. The Visitation of Norfolk in the Year 1563: Volume 2 - Page 51
19. The Historical Research Center, Irvine, California, USA
20. World Vital Records (http://www.worldvitalrecords.com/Thresten)
21. A Complete concordance to the works of Geoffrey Chaucer, Volume 14, Part 2 Volume 1 of Alpha-Omega: Englische Autoren A Complete Concordance to the Works of Geoffrey Chaucer Pages 513, 679 and 793

Websites

1. The Spencer Genealogy  By Jared L. Olar http://freepages.genealogy.rootsweb.ancestry.com/~fesscheq uy/Spencer.html
2. The History of Luzerne County Pennsylvania: http://www.usgwarchives.net/pa/luzerne/1893hist/1893bios/ 93co-cu.htm
3. WinstonChurchill.org http://www.winstonchurchill.org/
4. WYOMING COUNTY MARRIAGES AND DEATHS (AND OTHERS): http://www.pagenweb.org/~luzerne/wyoming/marriage1.ht m
5. The Drake Family: http://familytreemaker.genealogy.com/users/h/a/r/Ken-Hartke/BOOK-0001/0009-0001.html

6. Pennsylvania Genealogy http://pennsylvania-genealogy.net/Plymouth-in-Luzerne-County-Genealogy.cfm
7. World Vital Records: http://www.worldvitalrecords.com/GlobalSearch.aspx?qt=census&zln=threston&zdater=0
8. Len "Butch" Thresten (St. Vincent's Basketball): Dominating the hoops - Arts & Living - Citizens' Voice http://citizensvoice.com/arts-living/dominating-the-hoops-1.1087294
9. Contested Election Case of George McLean V. Charles C. Bowman: From the Eleventh Congressional District of Pennsylvania. John Thresten (Witness).

## Supporting Materials

1. Daily Life In Tutor England by Tim Lambert http://www.localhistories.org/tudor.html (Used as a reference for life and lifestyles in the 16th Century)

www.ingramcontent.com/pod-product-compliance
Lightning Source LLC
Chambersburg PA
CBHW071025040426
42443CB00007B/941